APHORISMS
MEDLEY OF THOUGHTS

APHORISMS

MEDLEY of THOUGHTS

by a Roving Philosopher

CHARLES HAAS

PHILOSOPHICAL LIBRARY
New York

To Andrée
who inspired all my thoughts of love

INTRODUCTION

The following 520 thoughts have been loosely classified according to different subject matter; all numbers ending in *1* would come under LOVE, 1, 11, 171, etc., all numbers ending in *7* could be classified under PHILOSOPHY, 7, 77, 297, etc.

1. LOVE

2. ECONOMICS

3. BEAUTY

4. PSYCHOLOGY

5. EDUCATION

6. WOMEN

7. PHILOSOPHY

8. SOCIOLOGY

9. WITTICISMS

10. MISCELLANEOUS

APHORISMS
MEDLEY OF THOUGHTS

1. College boy to pretty coed:
   "You love me."
   "How can you say such a silly thing. I hardly know you."
   "It is an undeniable fact. I can prove it with a syllogism.
   1. I love you, thus I am a lover;
   2. Everybody loves a lover.
   3. You are a part of everybody, therefore you love me."

   *　　*

2. There might be too many people on earth; for a merchant, however, there are never enough customers.

   *　　*

3. A teen-age girl is like a cactus orchid: beautiful to look at but not to be approached.

   *　　*

4. By concentrating minutely on one's self, one is prone to become a MEist.

   *　　*

5. Teaching courage, honor and love is more important than teaching all the sciences combined.

   *　　*

6. The ideal woman, by her simple presence, transforms this earth into a paradise.

7. "Are you for or against it?"
"I pride myself in being a philosopher, and like to look at all sides of a question: yours, mine, and the unbiased side. I am for or against anything only when I am wearing a uniform."

* *

8. History can be written different ways:
   1. Joan of Arc heard voices.
   2. Joan of Arc believed to have heard voices.
   3. One day Joan of Arc came home and told her father that she had heard voices.

* *

9. An efficiency expert replaced pencils in the office, because the secretaries spent too much time sharpening them. Each girl received a mechanical pencil for which she would have to pay if she were to lose it. Now the girls can be seen spending three times more time, walking from desk to desk asking each other: "Have you seen my pencil?"

* *

10. "Everything is sex," says the Freudian addict. "The beauty of the flowers in spring, the enchantment of the songs of birds, all are nothing but the invitation to procreation."
"Some of us poets are strange people, we refuse to admit such thoughts, we call them just ugly."

* *

11. A psychologist told me: "Look out for number one." He even tried to prove to me that I was the most important person to myself. He is completely wrong. The most important person in the world to me is the person I love.

12. In the spring the fields are covered with grass; each square inch is so densely filled that it seems impossible for anything else to grow there. One month later these same fields are white with daisies. A young man finishing his education should keep this in mind when he is looking for a job.

* *

13. Physical beauty changes quickly into ugliness if it is not accompanied by moral beauty.

* *

14. Only what you do not like to do is difficult to do.

* *

15. "Son, you are free to direct your admiration towards the morning dewdrop on the velvet petal of a crimson rose, or toward a harlot dancing in the raw."

* *

16. A woman who does not acknowledge a gentleman's polite gestures, might kill his sense of chivalry.

* *

17. "It says in the history book that Socrates asked questions. Therefore he was condemned to death," says the young student. "What kind of questions did he ask?"
The old teacher is smiling:
"Here is an example: Who is more important to you, the garbage collector or the king?"
"The king, of course!" retorts the young man.
"If both were to go away for a month, and nobody would replace them, who would be missed more?"

"The garbage collector, of course."
"Then, who is the more important of the two?"
"The garbage collector," grumbles the student.

*   *

18. After the end of a civilization there are usually more people alive than when it began.

*   *

19. "As I advance in years, I realize more and more that not all opinions different from mine are necessarily wrong."

*   *

20. There are people who, having been repeatedly stung by the thorns of a rose bush, can no longer see the beauty of the flower nor smell its fragrance.

*   *

21. In poor countries a boy shows his love for a girl by writing her a poem. In rich countries he buys her a present.

*   *

22. The imperialist says: "Let us pay the least for the most." The ambassador of good will says: "Let us pay the most for the least."

*   *

23. God creates beautiful rocks, but human hands must polish a rough stone into a sparkling jewel.

24. "Give me a hamburger, that's the only good food there is," says the man who identifies a certain dish with carefree parties. When he feels out of place in new surroundings, he trusts that that certain dish will bring with it a joyful mood.

*   *

25. Education should: (Among other obvious things)
    1. Teach the difference between good and bad;
    2. Develop the intellect;
    3. Make us aware of beauty around us.

*   *

26. "When I was young, women took my covetous glances for smiles of admiration," says the old philosopher. "Now they take my smiles of admiration for covetous glances."

*   *

27. An opinion is of value only if it either awakens your spirit of contradiction, or if it substantiates your preconceived notions; it should not leave you indifferent.

*   *

28. Several hundred thousand years ago, cavemen drew pictures on the walls. Since then man has advanced to incredible heights. Yet, till now, no animal can do what cavemen did so long ago. What has happened to evolution, as explained by Darwin?

*   *

29. A Syllogism:
    A. A gentleman believes in woman's intuition.
    B. A scientist does not.
    C. A scientist is no gentleman.

5

30. In a boxing ring, only the fighters get hurt; sometimes accidentally, the referee. In an atomic war, however, the spectators become part of the fight.

*   *

31. "We are made for each other," is a cliché based on hope. The real test of lasting love is to state, after years of happiness: "We have made each other for each other."

*   *

32. While most European nations looked for markets all over the world, the United States of America found a ready market for its surplus goods among the poor people at home.

*   *

33. A beautiful ideal is like a white cloud around the peak of a high mountain. If you should ever reach it, you would find yourself in a fog.

*   *

34. Some people travel around the world to escape they don't know what, find nothing, and come back disappointed.

*   *

35. Emphasis on courtesy should be the principal aim in education.

*   *

36. A victim of efficiency is today's girl who talks only to a prospective husband, refusing to even smile at any other man.

37. It is more glorious to suffer misery in companionship for a noble cause than to revel in luxury alone.

* *

38. *A*nalysis *B*efore *C*riticism is the ABC of democracy.

* *

39. A certain "expert" on bird life tells us that birds sing only when they are suffering. Do we, ignorant poets, have to be ashamed now, when we are enjoying the song of a bird?

* *

40. "Who started the fight?" asks the child. "Whoever did, is guilty."
"What was the fight all about?" asks the adult. "And what started it?"

* *

41. She: "What can I give you to show that I love you?"
He: "Your company."

* *

42. The possession of tangible riches and comfort of the aristocracy, the leisure time of the nobility, and the refinement of society have been the envy of the multitudes for centuries. Now capitalism has brought comfort and leisure to all.

* *

43. Young man to his beautiful girl friend:
"Wherever you are
Is my Shangri-La."

44.   Wars and evil deeds are blamed on human nature, love never.

*   *

45.   Father to 14 year old son:
      "Which profession would you like to follow?"
      "I'd like to do what I want."
      "How do you know that what you want today will be the
         same thing you will want tomorrow, or next year? Two
         years ago you wanted to become a fireman. Last year a
         private eye."
      "I want to be an engineer."
      "Then you have to study lots of mathematics."
      "I hate mathematics."
      "I think you are too young to know what you want."

*   *

46.   Girls become pretty ugly when they behave like men.

*   *

47.   "What is a philosopher?"
      "It's a man who talks about anything that's none of his
         business."
      "You mean the opposite of an expert?"
      "You might call it that. An expert knows everything about
         one thing, and when he talks about that one thing, every-
         body shuts up. A philosopher knows just one thing about
         everything, and everybody can add his two cents worth to a
         discussion with him. He does not know everything about
         any one thing."

*   *

48. The country about which we read in history books, is not the country in which we are living today.

*   *

49. "Don't be a psychologist who asks: 'Who was speaking?' Be a philosopher and ask: 'What did the man say?'"

*   *

50. If you don't like snails because you have never eaten any, you have no right to say that they don't taste good.

*   *

51. What is love?
Young love: The swain goes down on his knee and declares his love.
Married love: Before the husband can kneel down to express his love, his wife says: "Let me place a handkerchief on the floor. You are going to get your pants dirty."
Old Love: The wife places a cushion on the floor to soften the fall, when her old husband kneels down to declare his everlasting love.

*   *

52. Money is stronger than the sword.

*   *

53. The five senses of beauty are: sight, hearing, touch, smell, and taste.

*   *

54. "I am an old man; I have my habits. . . ."

55. The difference between a high school pupil and a college student can be noticed by the statements they make:
"Teacher, you give us too much homework."
"Professor, you don't give us enough homework."

* *

56. A lady is never comfortable.

* *

57. "There is nothing new in the world," is a partial truth, that is to say a complete lie. Every time I hear something I have never heard before, it is completely new to me, even if it is 3000 years old. A person who does not know Plato's Cave Theorem, will find it new when he hears it for the first time.

* *

58. Symbols of different eras:
    1. Religion — crusades.
    2. Nation — wars of glory for country.
    3. Freedom — wars of liberation.

* *

59. Advertizers soon realize that people do not believe everything they are told about a certain product. When, however, opinions about certain abstract subjects are voiced, some lawmakers are convinced that the public is very gullible and should not be exposed to "dangerous" ideas.

* *

60. "Why did he do that to me?"
"If you want to know, you'll have to take time to find out. Once you find out, you'll forgive him. So, why not forgive him right now?"

61. After having read the description of a thing, one can only be disappointed when meeting it; the only exception to this rule is love. It has never been described to fit the emotions of a person in love.

* *

62. Today new machines are needed much more to fight the worker's boredom than to lessen his manual labor.

* *

63. When you have too much of any one thing, you can no longer find it beautiful, no matter what it is.

* *

64. An artist may either try to impress other artists, or he may try to communicate with the general public.

* *

65. "If there were only one sentiment you could teach your son, let it be enthusiasm."

* *

66. Charm and kindness cannot be the weapons of a woman.

* *

67. The description of life, devoid of any feeling, is atrocious.

* *

68. History has often been classified into centuries:
    17th century: Establishing nations;
    18th century: Intellectualism;
    19th century: Colonialism;
    20th century: Individual comfort.

11

69. "You can't fight progress!" shouts the young man who is trying to sell something nobody wants.

* *

70. "This has been done before."
"Everything has been done before, but that does not mean that we should not do it again. After all, you have eaten before. . . ."

* *

71. A short declaration of love:
"Let us build a life together."

* *

72. Around the turn of the century, efficiency experts tried to extract the maximum out of each worker. More and more machines came to replace workers. Now workers are often only watchers of machines who produce the maximum needed. Now all that efficiency experts can do, is to make the work a pleasure for the workers.

* *

73. A prostitute can not be beautiful. There is no esthetic beauty without moral beauty to go with it.

* *

74. The most disliked person is the one who refuses our charity.

* *

75. Education means to lead children out of childhood.

76. The smile of a sales girl is inversely proportionate to her experience.

* *

77. "My hobby is my job."
"You are a real success in life."

* *

78. "Fais de ton mieux
Dans ton propre milieu."
(Do your best in your own crowd)

* *

79. With television in the home, speaking is becoming more and more difficult. Some old saying will have to be changed from: "That is easier said than done," to "That is easier done than said."

* *

80. You don't tell a news reporter that he wrote a good article any more than you would tell a bus driver that he has driven his bus well.

* *

81. Any activity without love becomes boring.

* *

82. Budget balancers are enemies of prosperity.

13

83. If you cannot afford to surround yourself with beautiful works of art, it is very important that you learn to enjoy eating, drinking, and talking with friends.

*   *

84. It would hurt us to find out that the person we feel sorry for, actually feels sorry for us.

*   *

85. Everybody seems to know how to raise other peoples' children.

*   *

86. Résumés of plays, short half-hour versions of novels, force the writer to eliminate any person or character who will not become familiar with the hero or heroine. If this spirit is carried into everyday life, when a married man is seen talking to another woman, tongues begin to wag, and he is accused of adultery.

*   *

87. Truth is often just interpretation of facts. To each his own way of interpreting.

*   *

88. Institutions may be organized, but society organizes itself.

*   *

89. "He is a very intelligent man; his ideas are the same as mine," smiles the MEist.

90. Pride is found in doing something difficult.

* *

91. "You don't have to make yourself pretty, you are," says the young lover.

* *

92. Trade means selling for those who sell.

* *

93. Many people apply the "New Car" philosophy to all phases of life. It is based on the publicity which surrounds a new car; nothing is as great, as marvellous, as beautiful as a new car . . . (until the next year's model comes out of the factory, that is to say.)

* *

94. It is the brotherly urge to bestow upon others the pleasures as we enjoy them. It hardly ever occurs to us, that others may be happy in their own way.

* *

95. "My aim in life is that of becoming a gentleman," announces the student of literature.

* *

96. A large family is usually a group of people where arguing is going on continuously. A girl from such a family will want to argue with someone in her mature years. Her husband who comes from a small family, does not always realize that his wife is just arguing because she is feeling young, and that she is only trying to relive her "arguing" childhood.

15

97. Everybody may smoke, but only too few dare not to smoke.

*   *

98. A law enforcement officer who sees only the bad element of society is prone to classify *all* men as bad. He must be continuously on the alert that there are *good* people in this world, even if he does not meet any when on the job.

*   *

99. In time of war you may doubt the existence of God, but you are not permitted to doubt the validity of the judgement of a general.

*   *

100. When the job is a man's very life, and not just making a living, retirement is a coming down, not a glorious achievement for many people. To know how to live without working for a living is an achievement in itself.

*   *

101. That is an old, old story,
It happens ev'ry day.
There is no need to worry
If you just stay away.
But if it should strike you
And you become a part,
The story is all new
And simply breaks your heart.

*   *

102. A French farmer said that he has a richer harvest with direct hand labor than farmers with machines. "Besides," said he, "I could not sleep nights, knowing that I had chased young farm hands and their families into city slums."

103. When a learned person says: "I don't understand the beauty of modern art," he is either ignorant, polite, or too cowardly to defy a cult.

* *

104. "Knowing the cause of a mental quirk will give us a solution," is a wrong premise. It is just like stating that, "Finding the cause of the fire will help us extinguish it."

* *

105. There are two ways of learning:
1. Learning to do.
2. Learning to like to do.

* *

106. "I am a worker, not a woman and I dress accordingly," says many a modern girl. "I am a woman only when I go out at night with my boy friend; then I also dress accordingly."

* *

107. Many a critic of art sees only the good, or he does not talk about it. He does not want to hurt the feelings of a small group of people. Some critics see the good as well as the bad, and they mention both. Who does the most good for the greatest number of prospective spectators?

* *

108. It takes more courage for a high school boy to do something and be called "a coward," than it takes to go hunting lions in Africa.

17

109. Proportionately, the least used object in the world is the fire extinguisher.

* *

110. The old married man has no right to tell a young couple that cleaning the fireplace is a terrible chore. The young couple's ideal of life might be sitting quietly in the living room, listening to the crackling of burning wood in the fireplace.

* *

111. "What is charm?"
"A myriad of I don't know which undefinable qualities."

* *

112. When there is no more room for advancement in some business concern, the older worker is told to retire on account of his age. Such a lie needs to be changed to: "You have had your glory. Give a young man a chance to do what you have done."

* *

113. "J'accepte le beau du nouveau,
Si c'est mieux que le vieux."
(I accept the beautiful of the new,
If it is better than the old.)

* *

114. Boredom of work for eight hours a day creates the fanatic urge "to get it over with."

* *

115. An educated person can entertain a new idea, someone else, and himself.

116. For a loving husband, every other woman is a "hot potato."

* *

117. A defeat which you refuse to accept is the beginning of a victory.

* *

118. Throughout the ages when bad things used to happen often, it was wise to be a pessimist.

* *

119. "Bah! Politics!" shouts many a man who is successful in politics.

* *

120. A pleasure can be multiplied by dividing it.

* *

121. That man loves his wife so much, that she is afraid to look at any object for fear that he buy it for her, and thus spend all the family income.

* *

122. "Diminish the people's confidence in the future, and you have a depression on hand," says the banker who knows his business.

* *

123. A visitor in a foreign country may admire the beautiful roses on the rosebush; he has no right to even notice the thorns.

124. The inevitable is often accepted as a matter of necessity; but only until the day when a way out is found. Then the inevitable becomes an unbearable burden.

* *

125. Teacher to his high school class: "I heard that you girls hardly eat anything when you eat together. I would like to make some research to know the number of chocolate bars girls carry in their handbags, to eat alone, between meals."
"That would not be research," answered one girl. "That would be snooping."

* *

126. What married women say about love to their husbands must forever remain a secret.

* *

127. Thoughts are of value according to their moment of need.

* *

128. We all lead three lives:
    1. private;
    2. professional;
    3. social.

* *

129. "Please let me hear an opinion contrary to my own," is a philosopher's motto.

* *

130. Before television came, a burial hearse was usually followed by 20 to 30 cars with their lights on in broad daylight. Now we hardly ever see more than 2 or 3 cars accompanying the departed on his last journey.

131. A business man looking at a loving couple;
"These two young people are ready for a merger."

*   *

132. The rich posts bail, the poor goes to jail.

*   *

133. The beautiful sound of rain drops falling in the garden is
music to the poet. Does the practical man no longer have
a right to listen calmly to the symphony of nature?

*   *

134. Everyman has at least three personalities:
1. What he thinks he is;
2. What others think he is;
3. What he really is.

*   *

135. What you can learn in two shakes of a lamb's tail, isn't worth
more than two shakes of a lamb's tail.

*   *

136. Instead of complaining: "She doesn't understand me," a
husband should say: "I don't understand her, but I am
going to try."

*   *

137. In every country there are some people who glorify the love
of power and others who glorify the power of love.

138. Freedom means the daily choice between good and bad. If there is a law against any thing bad, it is no longer a glory to be free. Then it is a crime not to be free.

*   *

139. When we hear about the over population of the world, it is so easy to suggest a lowering of the birth rate, in OTHER countries, that is to say. No public figure would suggest it at home.

*   *

140. A good novelist tries to unite scholarship and common sense.

*   *

141. You cannot help loving who loves you.

*   *

142. Efficiency experts have complied with the businessman's request of doing skilled work with unskilled labor, by making each worker skilled in one minute operation. The end justifies the means, is the guiding principle of many a business.

*   *

143. When talking about our country to a fellow citizen, we see only the bad things. When talking to a foreigner, we see only beauty and perfection everywhere.

*   *

144. The fulfilment of a wish creates another wish. Prosperity can thus be built on continuous wish-fulfilment.

145. Character is developed by doing what you don't like to do.

* *

146. Since advertisers continuously tell women that dishes wash themselves with the latest detergent or soap, many women now use paper plates and keep their beautiful Haviland dishes forever hidden in the china closet.

* *

147. En temps de loisir
Il faut savoir agir.
(In leisure time one must know how to act.)

* *

148. Signatures are illegible in countries where people have no bank accounts.

* *

149. Many an "Expert" is but a squelcher of dreams.

* *

150. Living with a problem is just as good, if not better, than solving it too rapidly. We cannot live without problems; each time one is solved another appears on the horizon.

* *

151. Washing dishes for one's beloved, in an era when washing dishes is a degrading chore, is a sign of love.

* *

152. Economic security has diminished the need of praying for one's daily bread.

153. "Did you ask a boy to ask you to the Sadie Hawkins dance?"
"Why, *professor*, do you think it is nice for a girl to ask a boy to take her to a dance?" answered the old-fashioned, well-mannered and really beautiful girl.

* *

154. Youth is called courageous when it is just acting normally: it does not yet know fear.

* *

155. "You need the three Ps, — Pencil, Pen and Paper — and you must practice the three Ss — Spelling and Sitting Still — if you want to learn the three Rs — Reading, 'Riting and 'Rithmetic" — announced the elementary school teacher.

* *

156. Fear and worry are part of most women's make-up.

* *

157. Every follower of a great leader is a leader in his small circle, but he is as essential as the great leader himself.

* *

158. Through generalizations we form our concepts of history which are very romantic but rarely true to life.
When we speak only about the gladiators killing each other, we forget that 500,000 to one million decent citizens lived in Rome at the time.
A few notorious criminals have given Chicagoans such a bad name that they cannot travel to Europe with a violin case without being looked upon with suspicion.

By talking only about the era of concentration camps in Germany, we forget the eighty million hard working, honest people.

* *

159. "Here are my conclusions upon which we are going to base our facts. If we don't have any facts, let's get some," says the aggressive executive.

* *

160. By being anxious to learn all the bad news in far away places, it is easy to become ignorant of what is going on in one's own neighborhood.

* *

161. A man does not need to worry about what is ahead, when he has a loving wife alongside of him.

* *

162. It is the bosses' job to find work for their workers.

* *

163. Beauty of memory is the exchange of nostalgic souvenirs.

* *

164. Brothers and sisters are continuously insulting each other, lest they arouse tender feelings for each other.

* *

165. "There is nothing new in the world," sounds strange to a school teacher. In school, students want to hear something new each day, even if it is very old to the teacher.

166. Ce qui est honteux, attire les yeux.
(That which is shameful attracts the eyes.)

* *

167. Adventure is the conscious contact with the unknown.

* *

168. A problem can be either a burden or a challenge.

* *

169. Descartes said: "I think therefore I am." A practical man might say: "I am, therefore I must eat, sleep, and think once in a while."

* *

170. The less you do, the more each action becomes painful.

* *

171. Nationalism is the first religion of any nation. In time of war, even the clergy has to ignore the famous command of Jesus Christ: "Love thy neighbor!"

* *

172. "In order to maintain prosperity, people must be trained to want to buy everything they see. Youth must be educated in the love of manufactured articles, not in love of nature." This is a well meaning economist's point of view.

* *

173. Most all inventions used in daily life today went through three stages: need, comfort, beauty.

174. The one who calls the daily routine: the daily grind, is destined for a life of eternal boredom.

* *

175. Will-power or the control of oneself must be practiced in school. Three ingredients are necessary for success: ability, time and will.

* *

176. Some women often talk about no longer having their pet dog, and of the day it died. They never speak about the many years of joy it brought them.

* *

177. Many people escape by means of books or plays into a world in which they would not want to live, much less be seen by an acquaintance.

* *

178. "If I say that Paris is a beautiful city, I do not mean that my home-town here in America is not also beautiful."

* *

179. In general, newspapers point out the rotten trees in a beautiful forest.

* *

180. Some people think: "A mechanic is more skilled than I, he can repair a car. I am more intelligent than he, in my own field."

181. "I am free. I am not married."
"You mean you can cry in your beer, Sunday morning at a bar counter."

*   *

182. Misery may be caused by the need of essential things such as a new car, a good job, the knowledge of Plato's Republic. . . .

*   *

183. Being aware of the beautiful is an art which may be learned by every one.

*   *

184. Some people call psychology: simple ideas shrouded in technical jargon.

*   *

185. Language study without grammar is like playing music by ear; you soon become tired of it.

*   *

186. Just as many girl visitors see only the dust in other peoples' homes, so many tourists see only the dirt in other cities.

*   *

187. There are three points of an idea:
1. What you say;
2. How you say it;
3. Why you say it.

188. The Wild-West was a one-way picnic.

* *

189. "It is easy for me to love humanity, but difficult, nay, impossible, to love my neighbor," grumbles the cynic.

* *

190. "Where can one use freedom of speech? Those who have the means of disseminating ideas are too well organized to permit a newcomer to say something they do not like," says the author who cannot find a publisher for his book.

* *

191. "We don't want science to take away from us our belief that rats abandon the ship which is doomed," says the old sailor. "We like rats, for as long as they are aboard, we are sure of coming home safely."

* *

192. Increased production caused the advertizing elite of today. Once there was too much merchandise on the shelves, someone had to come and sell it.

* *

193. Art today is in the hands of the businessman. The average man finds more pleasure in looking at the beautiful ads in the magazines, than in searching for beauty in what is called modern art.

* *

194. The disease of the twentieth century is the analysis of one's self, specializing in this activity so much, that we have no more time to look around us, up to the Infinite.

195. What you learn in school does not matter as much as how you learn it.

* *

196. Civilized man wants to see of women one inch more than he can see.

* *

197. Evil makes us cognizant of the existence of good. If there were no thieves, we would not realize that there are many, many honest people around.

* *

198. What may be good in Hollywood, may be taboo in Timbuktu.

* *

199. "I have reached the age where I catch cold easier, where I have a backache once in a while, and where I wear long underwear in winter."

* *

200. We should not confuse freedom of speech with the right to obscene swearing, even if it is supposed to make bestsellers. It is actually sacrilegious to mention our glorious freedom to excuse an ill-mannered word or gesture.

* *

201. "The classics ornate the shelves in my livingroom. I might never have the time to read them all, but I like to show my respect for them."

202. By high standard of living some people mean a high standard of morals.

* *

203. Ugliness, just as beauty, is only skin-deep.

* *

204. Suicide is sometimes an easier way out than being confronted with a dilemma for a while.

* *

205. "Just because you can play Liszt's Second Rhapsody, doesn't mean that you should stop playing the piano," says the teacher to the student.

* *

206. A twentieth century serenade is the tooting horn of a car in front of a girl's house.

* *

207. No man believes a lie, as long as he is convinced that what he believes is the truth.

* *

208. In many countries young college students stage demonstrations against established conditions. When these boys grow up, they will fight for the established conditions against the college students.

31

209. "Where do you get these cock-eyed ideas? They are so different from mine."

*   *

210. If you travel by plane, you are only leaving and arriving, not traveling at all.

*   *   '   '

211. "I do not want to taste your caviar."
"Why not?"
"If I should like it, I would be sad for the rest of my days, because I could not afford to buy it."

*   *

212. The basic need of a high school girl is a new dress for each school day.

*   *

213. The climate in the tropics is too hot for the tourist to even notice the beauty of palm trees on the sandy beaches.

*   *

214. Bored people feel persecuted.

*   *

215. "You don't go to school to learn, son, you go there to study. Learning is the result of studying."

*   *

216. A lady chews gum only when she is repairing her car behind her garage.

217. "That dog bit my boy. It must be shot!" shouts the angry father.
"Are you sure the dog was mad?" Socrates would ask.

*   *

218. An important event may actually be publicized into insignificance.

*   *

219. "A question I cannot answer is a silly question," says the MEist.

*   *

220. No one is more skeptical than a scientist, he can only believe something which is an irrefutable fact.

*   *

221. "Do you know how rich I am?"
"You don't need to be admired by anybody else; you are doing that very well yourself."

*   *

222. Lots of money is needed to fight boredom.

*   *

223. "What is beauty?"
"The object you like."

*   *

224. The art of painting has become a subject of psychoanalysis. To know how the artist got his inspiration is more important than the painting itself.

225. A well educated man has the ability to make life pleasant for those around him.

* *

226. The type of woman who catches the eye of a professional photographer is not typical.

* *

227. Pleasure is not happiness. Only work well done gives satisfaction and happiness.

* *

228. There are two sorts of poor people: those who have nothing, and those who appreciate nothing.

* *

229. Freedom of speech is fine, but don't you dare to mention the word "BOMB" near an airplane. Our law makers think that we are all dumb and become hysterical. Some citizens feel insulted.

* *

230. If we are judged by what we read in the daily papers, we are the worst nation in the whole world.

* *

231. What happened to the love of our fellow man during the Second World War? We heard a song with the title: "Praise the Lord and Pass the Ammunition."

232. Men's ties are chosen by their wives, relatives, secretaries and given as presents.

* *

233. It is the small black spot on the white tablecloth which makes the beauty of the whole disappear.

* *

234. Only what you do not like to do is difficult to undertake and to accomplish.

* *

235. It's for you to choose! Anything, good as well as bad, that you do three times with pleasure is prone to become a habit.

* *

236. Here is a sentence for practicing the French *U* sound: (Not for high school use.)
On admire les statues de femmes nues,
Mais une femme nue, qui remue,
N'est pas une statue.
(Statues of nude women are admired, but a nude woman who moves is not a statue.)

* *

237. The elite is disappearing in proportion to the illiteracy of the general public.

* *

238. Religion used to give us a means to contemplate. Nowadays, in this busy world, contemplation is considered a waste of time.

239. "What kind of a father would give his son the first name of Attila?"
"Only a Hungarian."

* *

240. Newspapers, though they are talking about daily events, do not describe the times in which we are living. Present day life does not consist only of accidents, murders, divorces, suicides. . . . Happy events are occurring hundred times more often. There is love, happiness, lasting marriages, economic well-being. . . .

* *

241. You cannot love what you fear.

* *

242. Money is like health: you only miss it when you don't have it any more.

* *

243. For some people doodling is an art, for others it is not. Each one has a right to his opinion.

* *

244. Only the mind of the military can say: "I have to sacrifice a thousand lives today, so that, if my calculations are right, I can save ten thousand lives tomorrow."

* *

245. Today we are taught, and we believe that it is right, to be cowards when a man with a gun enters the room and shouts: "This is a hold-up!"

246. An attached, honest man must not give hope to a young unmarried woman. If he does, he is a heel.

* *

247. People who are traveling in an automobile, are actually living on an island inhabited only by its passengers.

* *

248. Civilization is the concrete, material progress. Culture is the mental, spiritual progress.

* *

249. "Time is Money," is a wrong statement when taken literally. The one who has time, has no money, he is a bum and the one who has money, has no time, he is too busy making more.

* *

250. 1. Pioneers, discoverers go out to find riches.
2. Pioneers, travellers just go.
Which of these opinions is yours?

* *

251. Life is a "ball" when it is filled with Beauty, Adventure, Love, and Leisure time.

* *

252. When prosperity exists in an atmosphere of war, it is better to call the period cold war, even if peace reigns. "Hot" peace may cause a depression.

253. A resting cat is a living statue.

*　*

254. Within a hundred years people will probably be flying to work in their armchairs, we are told. Are we now supposed to feel miserable because we still have to drive in our car and stay on the road?

*　*

255. Reading is the main way of learning something to say.

*　*

256. To a fanatic Freudian, a woman's radiant smile is nothing but the lewd grin of sexual desire; the sparkling eyes of a sweet, sixteen year old girl, nothing but the nascent urge to procreate the species. To a poet, to any honorable man, the radiant smile of a beautiful woman and the sparkling eyes of a young girl are the most glorious aspects of nature.

*　*

257. There are no partial truths: one cannot be partly man, woman; alive, dead; virgin or pregnant.

*　*

258. When we hear of an era in history described with a certain slogan, we should not forget that the slogan refers to the appearance of a certain phenomenon, to which only a few people adhered. The large majority of the people continued living in their own way, disregarding completely what the slogan suggested.

259. If you knew which parts of the animal go into a hot dog, you might not like hot dogs anymore.

* *

260. In some countries freedom means the freedom to starve to death. And who would want that?

* *

261. The pet in one's home is often given human qualities; he or she is loving, intelligent, sensitive. The man one knows is often called dumb, selfish, egotistical. That is to show, that the more we know an animal, the more human it becomes and the more we know man, the more like an animal does he become.

* *

262. "I wish I had a lot of money."
"What for?" asked the philosopher.
"What a silly question. Let's see. Gee, I have everything money can buy. . . . I am just afraid if something bad should happen."
"You don't need any money. You need confidence in tomorrow."

* *

263. Lasting beauty is a misnomer.
The beauty of what one loves is only there when one is aware of it. Beauty is a continuously recurring sensation.

* *

264. Maids have disappeared from the 20th century household. It had become too easy for maids to accuse their rich employer of the pregnancy they had incurred somewhere.

265. Many a college professor plays hooky. He makes elaborate plans for writing a book, but each time he is supposed to sit down and write, he finds something to do, which, for that very moment, seems more important to him. He thus never gets his book on paper.

* *

266. Experience often obliterates the smile of a waitress.

* *

267. It does not matter WHO is right, but WHAT. That is philosophy.
It does not matter WHAT is said, but WHO said it. That is psychology.

* *

268. It was at the end of the Second World War that a new law was enacted, i.e. Leaders of losing nations became war criminals.

* *

269. Textbooks about Sigmund Freud are the only ones professors read nostalgically, college boys droolingly, and coeds "gigglingly."

* *

270. Once you know success, and you are on top, you'll find out that it is cold up there.

* *

271. No man is really wise until he is kind and courteous.

272. A European cannot understand how the owner of a $10,000 automobile can enjoy eating an 18 cts. hamburger in a drive-in stand.

* *

273. There is a great difference between visiting a beautiful city and living in it for a long time.

* *

274. "When our cat was only three months old, he climbed the damask curtains in the living room, tore up the upholstery of the velvet divan, and scratched the hand which stroked him too roughly."
"Have him altered," suggested a Freudian.
"We thus took him to a veterinarian, and took IT back home. The next day, and for two more years, it climbed the damask curtains in the living room, tore up the upholstery of the velvet divan, and scratched the hand which stroked it too roughly."

* *

275. The ability to scoff at temptation is the mark of a cultured man.

* *

276. A gracious lady feels that she looks older when she tries to behave like a little girl.

* *

277. The less we know about a certain subject, the more we have to use our passion at the expense of our reason, when discussing it.

278. A country's bad deeds are usually blamed on the people. A nation's glorious deeds are attributed to its leaders, who thus become great.

* *

279. Which statement is the Truth?
A. After a war, there is usually a great religious revival.
B. After a war, those who preach "Love thy Neighbor" usually come out of hiding and start to preach again.

* *

280. The art of using the strength of the enemy is sometimes called mental jiu-jitsu.

* *

281. Liebe ist ein angenehmes Gefühl.
(Love is a pleasant feeling.)

* *

282. "Save time!" shouts the salesman of time-saving devices.
"What for?" asks the philosopher.
"What a silly question. Only a philosopher can answer that," replies the salesman.

* *

283. Only when a woman is conscious of her beauty does she like to be admired.

* *

284. Quand on est bien fatigué
Et qu'on peut se laisser aller,
On se croit au paradis.

Mais quand on n'est pas fatigué,
Et qu'on ne peut pas se reposer
On se meurt de soucis.
(If you are pretty tired, and you can relax you feel like in
paradise. But when you are not tired and you cannot
rest, you just die of worry.)

* *

285. It is not enough to get what you want, you must also want
what you get, and want what you wanted once you know
what it really is.

* *

286. Here is one woman's reasoning which seemed odd to a
practical man: "A cup of black coffee keeps me awake,
but when I add some cream, it puts me to sleep."

* *

287. "I don't smoke, therefore I do not miss a cigarette. Some
people do not enjoy the luxuries I do, but that does not
mean that they are less happy than I. They do not miss
the luxuries anymore than I miss the cigarette."

* *

288. "Why don't you have a United States of Europe as we
have a United States of America?"
The person who asks such a question should be reminded
that Europe is a continent, and that the "United States
of America" is a country. There is no United States of the
CONTINENT America, there are several independent
nations on this continent, like on the CONTINENT of
Europe.

289. "I used to like Philadelphia Pepperpot, until I found out that it contained tripe," said the man who had been a member of a political movement before it was outlawed.

* *

290. What a tourist should be looking for when traveling in a foreign land:
    1. How people eat;
    2. What kind of entertainment they have;
    3. How they spend their leisure time.

* *

291. There is no difference between an admiring look and a covetous stare; between gentle caressing and clumsy pawing. It all depends on the receiver.

* *

292. People can now buy optimism; i.e. they can take out an insurance on anything.

* *

293. If we are judged by the beautiful portraits which fill the pages of our magazines, we are the "smilingest," happiest people in the world.

* *

294. Rich people are living in a continuous struggle; they have to fight temptation every inch of their lives. They can buy all the food they wish, all the drinks they desire. If they should give in to those wishes they would all be fat as pigs, alcoholics. . . .

* *

295. In small groups the educated man agrees with the good he hears, but does not agree or disagree with the bad.

296. A boy is speaking about his girl friend:
"When she is losing at ping-pong, she can hardly bend down to pick up the ball when it falls on the ground. But when she is winning, she eagerly picks up all the balls, even her opponent's."

* *

297. "I always stick up for what is right."
"I am not always sure that what I think is right, *is* right," replies the philosopher.

* *

298. In times of peace, inhabitants of other countries are presented to us as hard working people, trying not to starve to death. In times of war, these same people, we are told, are blood thirsty monsters, eager to slice up any of our citizens.

* *

299. "That man does not know how to hide his learning; he is simply unbearable."

* *

300. As you travel through life, it might be a good thing to observe people around you and jot down what you see. When you read what you have written down, you might be surprised to notice that others have said what you have seen long before you. That does not make your observations less valuable, especially when they have been made by the great thinkers of the ages.

* *

301. J'ai passé mes vacances au pays
des heureux,

Ce royaume n'est peuplé que de
gens amoureux.
(I spent my vacation in the land of happy people. This
kingdom is inhabited only by people in love.)

*   *

302.   Whenever you kick, you are hurting someone.

*   *

303.   In later years we like to remember only the pleasant and
beautiful of every experience of the past.

*   *

304.   In order to be happy on the job, the attitude is more important
than the skill.

*   *

305.   It is not enough to speak a language, you must have something to say, not only in a foreign language but also in
your own.

*   *

306.   "Just shoot me and call me corpse," said the girl to the
employer who scolded her.

*   *

307.   The crisis of today is the scientific craze, or necessity — as
you wish, of classifying everything. It started with the
concrete: rocks, flowers, etc. and entered the abstract:
philosophy, art, literature and so on. Thus, great men
of today will be known to posterity only if they are
classifiable according to present day standards.

308. In a democratic nation the police does not fire machine gun bullets into demonstrating crowds.

* *

309. "I don't dare."
"If you have money and fame, you must dare."

* *

310. Integration means only intermarriage to some people.

* *

311. Love must come from an inward need.

* *

312. Machines have saved direct labor in most all enterprises. But those who make the machines, the secretaries, the advertisers, the comedians selling the product on the television are also working indirectly for the enterprise.

* *

313. Men are educated to admire the physical beauty of women. What are women trained to admire in men?

* *

314. "Do you happen to know where there is a barbershop around here?" asks a passerby.
"You seem to need a haircut yourself," replies the other man who had long hair.
"That is why I asked you."
"Oh, excuse me, I thought you were making fun of me."
That is what the passerby calls a me-ist.

315.   A high school girl confiding in her teacher;
"My parents think I cannot take care of myself."

*   *

316.   A girl soon finds out that when she dresses to accentuate
her physical attributes, she attracts the attention of older
or married men; only sometimes of younger men who,
however, look at her just as a passing fancy. When she
dresses decently, she will be noticed by decent young men;
and the others will not even look at her.

*   *

317.   Gründlichkeit und Gemütlichkeit
Bringen Glück und Zufriedenheit.
Gründlichkeit kann man erlernen.
Gemütlichkeit muss man erleben.
(Thoroughness and joviality
Bring happiness and contentment.
Thoroughness can be learned,
Joviality must be experienced.)

*   *

318.   There are forces in the world, which we cannot bend to obey
us and do what we want them to do.

*   *

319.   It is always amusing to hear people say coming out of a
theater: "I enjoyed the play very much, but it is not good
for the general public."
"Who *is the general public?* Is it not everybody? Or is it
everybody but you?"

*   *

320.   "Giving is nicer than receiving."
"That sounds nice," answered the rich man. "But nobody
around me needs anything, and I don't need anything
either."

321. The biggest problem a loving husband faces all his life, as he looks at his beloved wife, is to express the same deep feelings of love with new words.

* *

322. Today's federal budget deficit is like the Eiffel Tower in Paris. It was considered a monstrosity when it was built for a World's Fair. Now it is a permanent institution.

* *

323. To grow older means to change tastes, even as far as beauty is concerned.

* *

324. "Know thyself" was a suggestion by Socrates. It could mean: psychoanalyze yourself, or "Find out why you do not like to eat frog legs. If you should find out, I doubt that the knowledge will make you like frog legs from then on."

* *

325. A professor of English should not correct people outside of the classroom. After all, a doctor does not give advice for curing the cough of a person at a party.

* *

326. "She knows so many people that she actually doesn't know any."

* *

327. "And you mean to say that what we are decrying here is good?"
"Whether I think it is good or bad, is of no importance whatsoever. I couldn't change it if I wanted. We are just musing along."

328. History may be explained in quite different ways by a statesman, a military, a politician, a businessman, a romantic novelist, an astrologer, etc.

* *

329. How marvellous progress is! Now we have daily visitors in the form of television entertainers for whom we don't have to prepare a meal. There is no need for friends any more.

* *

330. Some old fashioned people still have the cult of quality.

* *

331. "Your wife is a very smart woman. She compliments you continuously," says the amateur psychologist.
"Is it not possible that she just loves me?" answers the philosopher.

* *

332. Without prosperity, democracy is on trial.

* *

333. "You are beautiful," says the gallant young man.
"What are you going to do about it?" replies the poorly educated girl.

* *

334. Leisure creates many an imaginary illness.

* *

335. "Let's get it over with!" is a dangerous slogan for high school children, when they are to take a summer class.

50

It is a state of mind which is carried over into college life where it is applied to every course not considered essential by the student. It is unfortunate when this state of mind persists after the college years and is applied to one's job.

* *

336. Some women see in the eyes of their dog things stranger than what a "connoisseur" of modern art sees in an abstract painting.

* *

337. Daily life in society is based on faith.
We go to a restaurant with faith that we will not be poisoned, and the restaurant owner has faith in us that we will pay for what he served us.
When we buy some gasoline, we have faith that the attendant will not fill our gasoline tank with water, and also he has faith that we will pay for what he puts into our tank.

* *

338. The degree of civilization of a victorious nation is often judged by the behavior of its soldiers in a vanquished country.

* *

339. When you have a foreign accent, you may talk about the country in which you are residing only in the form of a travelogue.

* *

340. You can get out of people only what you think about them.

341. The nicest way of acquiring callouses on one's hand is by applauding those who have done something for others.

* *

342. Today's creative person is the businessman who creates jobs.

* *

343. Do not complain that beautiful roses have thorns.

* *

344. Older men often do not realize that growing old means becoming more careful. Young people call that: being scared easily.

* *

345. There are two sorts of children in high school: students and "horse-players."

* *

346. For some women essential needs are the things they cannot afford to buy.

* *

347. The pleasure of discussing a problem ends, whenever a solution is found. So please, let us not find a solution too quickly.

* *

348. Only a gargoyle of Notre-Dame de Paris can look at history objectively.

349. "Money isn't everything," says the rich man who has so much of it, that he does not need anything anymore.

*   *

350. My living room becomes smaller each time I add another piece of furniture.

*   *

351. "Une fois qu'on t'a vue,
On ne t'oublie plus."
(Once you have been seen, one cannot forget you anymore.)

*   *

352. Hatred is sometimes used by leaders of a country to maintain prosperity.

*   *

353. "The morning dew drop on the velvet petal of a crimson rose, which used to make me gay, now makes me cry," says the poet who lost his love.

*   *

354. It is only when you know fear that your courageous action may be called courageous.

*   *

355. When you re-read a text book, you realize how much you already know.

*   *

356. The entrance of women in the Armed Forces has diminished the boys' enthusiasm for war.

357. Happy is the man for whom duty and pleasure are synonymous.

*   *

358. Christians were not killed in the Roman arenas because they practiced Christianity, but because they refused to adopt the religion of nationalism.

*   *

359. "Adventure is 99% discomfort and 1% danger," said the cynic.

*   *

360. A dictatorship is a land of opinions expressed inwardly only.

*   *

361. When a man is so imbued by the laws of good that he could not possibly want to do any evil, he is free to undertake anything he wants.

*   *

362. As economic security increases, the effectiveness of prayer cannot easily be tested.

*   *

363. A favorite dish is usually one to which beautiful memories are attached.

*   *

364. "I feel sorry for you."
"The same here."

365. "Boys will be noise."

In a classroom this can be remedied either by building a soundproof wall around the school or by teaching them to be quiet. The first way is the easiest one.

*　　*

366. If you agree with what a woman says, she may quote you as having said what she said. After all, you did not dare to contradict her.

*　　*

367. By eliminating most physical effort from manual labor or mental effort from office work, we have achieved something which cannot be dismissed with a shrug of the shoulders: workers now hate their jobs.

*　　*

368. Civilization means victory over inhuman desires in men.

*　　*

369. Anarchists are groups of people who love to suffer in joyous unison.

*　　*

370. Who does nothing for his friend will kill the friendship.

*　　*

371. "Tell me something pleasant: Kindness is more important than truth," states the old philosopher.

*　　*

372. In time of prosperity we can afford to see only the good everywhere.

373. Celui qui apprécie
Aime vraiment la vie.
(He who appreciates really loves life.)

*   *

374. "Think of yourself, first and always," announces the psychologist. "Analyze yourself, know your likes and dislikes." "Forget yourself," states the philosopher. "Think of others first. Learn about their likes and dislikes."

*   *

375. In order to make people vote for higher salaries for teachers, it seems necessary today to present the teacher as a poor, starving, underpaid beggar. Is it surprising that the teaching profession is not respected?

*   *

376. When a woman swears in mixed company, it is like a burp; some people find it cute, some find it ill-mannered.

*   *

377. A soldier is amoral during a battle only.

*   *

378. People are often collectively opposed to what they like individually, and vice versa.

*   *

379. "Travel means education," is a sweeping statement. If it were universally true, then sailors would be the best educated men speaking the most refined language. Immanuel Kant, on the other hand, who had never left his home town, should be considered as one of the least educated.

56

380. At many a social gathering of learned people, any allusion to a philosophical subject is avoided like the plague. Sport is less controversial.

* *

381. The love of beauty in music and art has been replaced by pride in the invention of the newest labor-saving device.

* *

382. Medicine can defy the forces that bring death. This causes overpopulation in poor countries. Medical science cannot do anything to prevent birth, that is not a scientific, but a religious matter.

* *

383. Art has spread out into many new fields in the twentieth century. A new automobile is an object of art. Not the creation of one individual, but the combination of the skills of many creative artists who collaborated in the creation of a useful object.

* *

384. "He was too young to be afraid of the future."

* *

385. Many people think they could write a book, if they had time. Few think that they could drive a school bus.

* *

386. "My life is certainly not monotonous; my wife does not always agree with me."

387. When you are tired of searching, you will come to believing without analyzing.

*   *

388. This age will someday be called, "The Age of the Superlative." We are trained to want the newest, the biggest, the best, of everything.

*   *

389. Prohibition in the United States of America was caused by the sudden prosperity of poor people. They had not learned how to use their leisure time before they had money to spare. Some of them spent their time gambling and drinking, coming home drunk and broke. Well-meaning persons began to decry drinking and passed a law against it. This in turn aroused a desire to drink in many people who had never thought about drinking before.

*   *

390. Some research results in an accumulation of technical jargon of use only to experts in the specific field.

*   *

391. Some people want money, others wisdom, others some one to love. Which is the best wish?

*   *

392. "Serve most people in the shortest time with the least help." That is the guiding light of efficient business.

*   *

393. The most beautiful aim in a young man's life is the continuous creation of memories.

394. Behavior describes a man more truthfully than his words.

* *

395. "Armchair" psychology is a pastime for those who do not read great books.

* *

396. "A woman should always look her best."
"I disagree. A woman should once in a while be less attractive. For everyday economic equality with man, she should not distract her fellow worker from his job, and make him lose it."

* *

397. By being raised with the imitation, one is often disappointed with the original.

* *

398. You must observe with the eyes of the specific time, if you expect to understand the customs of that certain period in history.

* *

399. Is: "The truth will set you free," a phrase which may be applied to a falsely condemned prisoner?

* *

400. Ideas of government usually follow trade.

* *

401. The sweetest moment in married life is making up after a quarrel. Quarrels are thus necessary, for, how else could the lovers enjoy making up?

402. MEist: "He must be suffering a monotonous existence; he does not enjoy life the same way I do."

*　　*

403. Self-esteem is created by doing something difficult.

*　　*

404. A person born blind does not suffer so much from his affliction, when compared with the person who became blind after an accident.

*　　*

405. The secret of success in the business world: Learn to appear busy at all times.

*　　*

406. A lady is a woman who gives a man an opportunity to be a gentleman.

*　　*

407. Aesop wrote his fables to illustrate his maxims.

*　　*

408. "The Survival of the Fittest," became a slogan and was used to justify the unethical behavior of certain businessmen as well as of some imperialistic governments.

*　　*

409. Today's civilization stresses that you be the opposite of what you are. The old want to be young, the young, old. The tall want to be shorter, the short, taller. The plump want to be slender, the skinny, plump. And to make everybody happy, you just call this discontent DIVINE.

410. A public speaker who speaks for the "masses," is usually a learned man who knows how to speak, wealthy enough to have ideas different from those of the multitude of his listeners.

* *

411. "Grass may be greener next door, but my grass is of the loveliest green shade in the world," says the happily married man.

* *

412. What is a capitalist? A millionaire or a small stock holder?

* *

413. Some authors find joy in describing the beauty of nature, tender feelings of lovers, deeds of kindness. Others relish in relating, in the name of "realism," the squalor of city slums, loathsome hatred or envy, crimes, etc. All this is reality, the ugly, as well as the beautiful.

* *

414. "Is there anything left with which you are not yet bored?" says the poet to the rich man, as they are walking side by side through a rose garden. "I feel sorry for you, despite all your wealth."

* *

415. "You must have an aim in life."
"Yes, I agree with you. But we change our aims so often."
"To improve one's self is an unchanging aim, I think."
"How can you improve yourself?"
"Re-read the classics."

416. Are we ready to let women support men?

* *

417. Occidentals: "We believe in lasting things, cathedrals, law books, constitutions. . . ."
Asiatics: "Our buildings may be blown away by the next hurricane."

* *

418. The "Mystery" in American history.
History books, historical novels and films depict the armed struggle between the early American settlers and the Indians fighting on horseback. The white men with superior arms were able to thus destroy the fighting Indians. But what happened to the women, the children and the oldsters?

* *

419. The unvarnished truth makes dull reading.

* *

420. A tourist should travel with an open mind, not only with open eyes.

* *

421. When a boy and a girl like to spend a whole hour, just talking, over a cup of coffee, they are really in love.

* *

422. To illustrate the fallacy of the theory "Supply and Demand" you may use the American woman's leg. When the Second World War came and there were no more silk stockings, nylon came into existence, and replaced silk with incredible speed and effectiveness.

62

423. Moral beauty is the only beauty which lasts forever, even if some people do not admire the advanced chronological age of a woman.

* *

424. A false accusation hurts more than the deepest physical wound.

* *

425. Language teacher to a prospective student:
"Do you want to study a language for three years so that you can take a rapid trip to a foreign country once in your life, and ask for a cup of coffee, or do you want to study the structure of the language and understand the beauty of the fine shades of meaning, the refinement of thoughts, the description of humanity, as written in the words of the geniuses of that language?"

* *

426. "Why did you smile at my child?"
That is how a passerby was scolded by a mother who has to share her child with television, phonograph, telephone, school, etc.

* *

427. "Do not become angry when a blind man bumps into you."

* *

428. Social relationship is mostly verbal exchange.

* *

429. Unless it is exceptional, it does not appear in the daily paper.

430. When an activity is no longer a challenge, most people just drop the whole thing.

* *

431. Many a rich man's son refuses to accept what his father wants to give him. His pride makes him cruel toward his parents who have worked all their lives with the one aim: "We wish to leave something worth-while for our son."

* *

432. "Those people are so backward, they have not yet any washing machines."
"Maybe *they don't* want any. Maybe they like to wash their clothes by hand and thus be useful to their family."
"They could do something else."
"What, for example?"
"I don't know. You are asking silly questions."
"You mean questions you cannot answer?"

* *

433. To arouse appreciation of the beauty in everyday life is the aim of literature.

* *

434. Most people accept their physical limitations, but not their intellectual ones. A man who is only five feet tall readily admits that he is not six feet tall, but he will hesitate to admit that there are some people around him who are more intelligent than he is.

* *

435. Things learned fast, don't last.

436. Mother visiting the young couple's home caused quite an uproar. She prevented the lawn from being watered, for fear that the birds would get their feet wet.

*　　*

437. When a mechanic shows what he knows, no one feels bad. When a professor who has studied for years tries to show some wisdom, people say that he is a show-off.

*　　*

438. A bear in a zoo is free. So is a goldfish in his bowl, and a canary in his cage. These are animals.

*　　*

439. The only "Thank You" one gets in a large city is the one printed on the check in a coffee-shop.

*　　*

440. When a 700 page book is condensed into one single sentence, its author is then identified with this one sentence.

*　　*

441. You are your brother's keeper only if he wants to be kept.

*　　*

442. Anonymous ownership of American business enterprises permits spending money before making any profit.

*　　*

443. The man who goes to work in the morning and likes it, is the poetry and beauty of every day life.

444. A "troublesome" mother-in-law is a mother who wants to help a young married couple that doesn't want to be helped. This is a normal situation in life. The well meaning mother reasons differently from her efficient businessman-son.

* *

445. Education has not brought us a multitude of geniuses as our forefathers had expected. It has done something much more important, it has made people kinder toward each other.

* *

446. Since the appearance of the ice box in the kitchen, a loving mother's problem has become: "How to get something into the children at dinner time." The children are hungry before mealtime, and insist on getting something out of the ice box, no matter how often the good mother says, "Wait till dinner." When dinner is finally called, the children have had so many snacks that they just aren't hungry, even when facing the most deliciously prepared meal.

* *

447. The disdain of the young for the old came when the young man went to school and soon knew more about abstract things than his practical, unschooled grandfather.

* *

448. A self made man is usually one who has helped others make themselves.

449. Advice to probationary teachers: (To be read aloud)
"You may disagree if you care,
But you won't be here next year."

*   *

450. He has that "What are we going to do next" attitude
of mind.

*   *

451. "Je veux être pour le reste de ma vie,
Ton amoureux, ton amant, ton mari."
(I want to be for the rest of my life,
Your sweetheart, your lover, your husband.)

*   *

452. "When you say a bad word about modern music, don't
you realize that you are hurting someone who tries to
make a living by playing such music?"

*   *

453. Teacher to a beautiful girl who wants a better grade:
"You deserve a bouquet of roses, but you do not deserve
a better grade in your studies."

*   *

454. Some of us are killing themselves trying to make their
lives easier.

*   *

455. Indifference creates ignorance.

456. Does an educated woman not have a right to a simple, yet so divine aim in life as a happy home, a loving husband, laughing children?

* *

457. "I did not win this argument, as you might think. During our discussion I have formulated several conclusions. You have contributed to the results as much as I," remarks the philosopher.

* *

458. Darwin created the concept that the fittest survive. This should not be considered an undeniable fact. Sardines, sheep, flies survive, while the large animals die out.

* *

459. The fear of a bogeyman defies scientific analysis.

* *

460. "He presents the exception as an example of the rule."

* *

461. Happy is the person who wants what he gets, and who loves it when he gets it. If he should not get what he wants, he learns to love what he gets.

* *

462. Taxes do not only go to business enterprises; they also go to workers in form of wages. Where else should the money from taxes go?

* *

463. "My son, even if it be true that if you ask you shall be given, do not forget to say 'Thank you' with a smile."

464. "Become ambitious, young man."
     "Do you mean, I should hate my job?"

* *

465. Teacher to pupil: "You certainly have improved this
     semester from a D grade to an A."
     "It is because you cracked down on me. That is the sign
     of a good teacher."

* *

466. Nowadays the girl often waits in her car for the boy to
     take her to a dance.

* *

467. Many people have espoused the "Paper-Cup" philosophy
     of life. Nothing is of lasting value.

* *

468. Civilization is the continuous creation of new desires;
     mostly forbidden fruit.

* *

469. When a man likes his work so much that he accepts his
     pay check sheepishly, we may call him a real success
     in life.

* *

470. Some people practice the art of seeing only the pleasant
     in life.

* *

471. The simple presence of one's beloved creates an atmos-
     phere of happiness.

472. The newspaper editor who mentions the national debt, is cutting his throat. He is scaring the public into buying less, which means less advertising for his paper, less income for his employees. Besides that, he is contributing to a depression.

*   *

473. Group entertainment and leisure time activity are more heartwarming and bring greater satisfaction than being entertained passively.

*   *

474. "If I were in his place, I would. . . ."
"You might place yourself in his shoes, but you are not he. His background, his make-up, his reactions are different from yours."

*   *

475. There are three sorts of growth:
1. vertical;   2. horizontal;   3. spiritual.

*   *

476. Girls chatting:
"If you count calories and eat only vegetables you won't gain any weight."
"How about cows, sheep, and elephants, they eat only vegetables they are certainly not slender, and they certainly don't count calories."
"What shall I do then to lose weight?"
"Eat anything you like, only less of it."

*   *

477. In time of war the power of reason is inversely proportionate to the waving of the flag.

70

478. There are different ways of knowing history: knowing what you should know and ignoring what you should not know.

* *

479. Let me illustrate the term Graded Equalization. Young girls use make-up to appear older. Grandmothers dye their hair to appear younger.

* *

480. "If you talk about understanding other people's behavior, you are talking shop; your profession being a novelist. I have a right to talk shop too. I am a deck hand and I know how to keep a deck clean," stated the old sailor.

* *

481. "How can I know that I really love my wife? I am twenty-two years old and we have been married for six months."
"Young man, you know that you love your wife, as soon as you can say that you love her in intimate privacy just as much as in society."

* *

482. During the seventeenth century kings had castles built along the Loire river in France. Was that luxury, or was it a way of giving jobs to workers, instead of building a war machine?

* *

483. The beauty of a smile is in the eyes, not only on the lips.

* *

484. Among adepts of psychology the discussion of ideas often changes into an analysis of personalities.

485. Maturity may be defined as consisting of:
    1. A sense of responsibility;
    2. Respect of others;
    3. The ability to endure adversity silently.

*   *

486. Mother to son: "We are going to visit the Joneses today. Promise me that you will not fight with their son Albert." "But what shall I do if he throws pepper in my eyes like the last time?"

*   *

487. You may either drink to get drunk or you may sip to loosen your tongue. The same way you may read to escape from your monotonous life or read to become a gentleman.

*   *

488. Meditation is an element of past civilizations. Today, every moment of life is usefully employed for work, television, and sleep.

*   *

489. What he thought was a sign of friendship, was only a salesman's smile.

*   *

490. An educational psychologist discusses principals, an educational philosopher discusses principles.

*   *

491. Love without sex is devine.
    Love with sex is human.
    Sex without love is animalistic.

492. In directing the public's eye away from the beautiful to the NEW, and avoid mentioning the word beautiful, the NEW will soon be identified with the BEAUTIFUL. Economists say often that that is an efficient way of molding public opinion. People are always ready to buy something new.

* *

493. Here is a definition of literature:
Literature is psychology embroidered with poetry.
It relates, in layman's language, problems which we might encounter in our own lives and their solutions.

* *

494. You are free to want anything, as long as you can handle it once you get it.

* *

495. The greatest joy a teacher can experience is when a girl student comes up to her and says:
"May I name my first child after you?"

* *

496. The twentieth century wife, whose home is stuffed with every conceivable modern convenience, to her husband:
"There is nothing left I can do for you."

* *

497. To feel the great movement behind a small event, an unimportant fact, a social condition, is called philosophy.

* *

498. "I don't want to change the world and I don't want the world to change me."

499. Killing a human being is a crime; in time of peace, that is.

* *

500. When an average man expresses a thought, he is sometimes reminded by an "expert" that, according to Plato, Socrates had said the same thing centuries ago. There might be several explanations of this:
   1. The man read and plagiarized Plato.
   2. He is a re-incarnation of Socrates.
   3. He has simply observed life around him and has come to his own conclusions, notwithstanding the observations of other men in the past.

* *

501. Your gift reflects your taste.

* *

502. During the Second World War unskilled labor produced the best warplanes.

* *

503. What is trash?
   Here are some definitions:
   Any book, no matter what subject it treats, which uses language no decent daily paper would lower itself to print.
   Any piece of printed matter which may not be sent by the United States mail, on account of its obscene language.
   Any book which a gentleman would not give to his lady friend on account of dirty language.

74

504. At a used car lot, the manager is addressing his sales
personnel:
"The car we have had standing around for six months,
was sold yesterday by Joe. It was worth $500.00. Joe
sold it for $600.00. He used PSYCHOLOGY!"
This word has acquired a new meaning. When a man
wants to sell something nobody wants to buy, he is
often told:
"You got to use psychology."

*　　*

505. "After you have read, you may sit down and write," was
the professor's advice.

*　　*

506. A young coed's inquiring mind should be exposed to
beautiful language, not lewd words in the name of
realism; to deep thoughts, not low ones; to worthy
objectives, not dirty ones.

*　　*

507. A lie may be a truth nobody wants to believe.

*　　*

508. Generalizations used for political expediency present a
constant danger in a democratic, free society.

*　　*

509. An "expert" might be able to prove that the "table d'hôte"
had been created for the travellers who insisted on eating
with the host, for fear that he might try to poison them
before stealing their belongings.
A poet would say that good companionship around the table
after a long day's journey through dust or rain, was
always a great delight.

510. The reasonable, cautious man seldom becomes a hero.

* *

511. A young college professor must be mentally neuter when making up the grades for his pretty coeds.

* *

512. A just deal is not just a deal.

* *

513. The beauty of a work of art and a good book defy the ravages of time.

* *

514. Interested people are interesting people.

* *

515. "Easy things are for morons," states the teacher. "And for them any mental effort is difficult."

* *

516. For some women, the dietician is a creator of forbidden fruit.

* *

517. In the material world there are inventors; in the abstract sphere of ideas there are only explorers and discoverers.

* *

518. Newspapers discuss the most realistic types of subject matter. Yet they don't seem to need obscene words to convey a spirit of "realism."

519. Youth is the happiest period in one's life, old people say. After all, it is life without any sense of responsibility.

*　　*

520. Throughout the Southern California landscape we find rows of ten to twelve eucalyptus trees. There are several explanations.
A. They were planted by some enterprising men for future lumber sales.
B. They were planted by some noble minded persons who wanted to build wind breakers and thus transform the desert into a fertile land.
Which explanation do you believe?

*　　*